Helping Children See Jesus

ISBN: 978-1-64104-023-5

Past, Present and Future of
God's Chosen People
Old Testament Volume 12:
Leviticus Part 2

Author: Arlene S. Piepgrass
Illustrator: Vernon Henkel
Colorization courtesy of Good Life Ministries
Page Layout: Patricia Pope

© 2019 Bible Visuals International
PO Box 153, Akron, PA 17501-0153
Phone: (717) 859-1131
www.biblevisuals.org

All rights reserved. No part of this publication may be reproduced, stored in a retrieval system or transmitted in any form by any means, electronic, mechanical, photocopy, recording or otherwise, without the prior permission of the publisher, except as provided by USA copyright law.

RELATED ITEMS

To access related items (such as activities, memory verse posters and translated texts) please visit our web store at www.biblevisuals.org and enter 2012 at the top right of the web page. You may need to reduce the zoom setting to get the search box.

FREE TEXT DOWNLOAD

To obtain a FREE printable copy of the English teaching text (PDF format) under Product Format, please scroll down and select Extra–PDF Teacher Text Download. Then under Language select English before clicking the ADD TO CART button to place in your shopping cart. Other languages are available at an additional cost from the Language menu. When checking out, use coupon code XTACSV17 at checkout and click on Apply Coupon to receive the discount on the English text.

I am the LORD your God . . . observe all My statutes, and all My judgments, and do them: I am the LORD.

Leviticus 19:36b, 37

Lesson 1
THE FEASTS OF THE LORD (Part 1)

> **NOTE TO THE TEACHER**
>
> These lessons together with Volume 11 of this series, form a unit. Both volumes will be more meaningful if they are taught after the five volumes of Exodus. The lessons in Exodus provide the historical background for the instructions given to Israel in Leviticus. These Leviticus lessons refer to incidents in Exodus, thus providing a good opportunity for review.
>
> Do you have a *New Scofield Reference* Bible? If so, study the notes on pages 156-158.
>
> In our previous study, we learned about God who is holy, a holy people, and holy places. Beginning with this lesson, we shall discuss the holy feast days which God ordered His people to observe.
>
> These feasts served two purposes: (1) They were constant reminders to Israel of God–who He is, and what He had done for them. (2) In advance, they gave a preview of the program of God. Many of these events have been fulfilled. Some, however, are still to occur.
>
> The specific dates mentioned in Scripture for the holy feasts are according to the Hebrew calendar. However, in these lessons, we are using approximate dates only.
>
> Review Volume 11 briefly. Discuss the offerings, the priests, the laws for daily living, and the Day of Atonement before beginning this lesson.

Scripture to be studied: Leviticus 23:1-14; Exodus 12; verses cited in lesson

The *aim* of the lesson: To show that God commanded Israel to observe specified days so they would remember regularly all He had done for them.

What your students should *know*: That God wanted His people to be thankful for His care, protection, provision and direction.

What your students should *feel*: Determined to live lives that honor the Lord.

What your students should *do*: Examine their lives and deal with the shortcomings that displease God.

Lesson outline (for the teacher's and students' notebooks):
1. The Sabbath (Leviticus 23:1-3; Genesis 2:1-3; Exodus 20:9-11; Nehemiah 13:15-18).
2. The Passover (Leviticus 23:4-5; Exodus 12:1-51; Deuteronomy 16:1-8).
3. The Feast of Unleavened Bread (Leviticus 23:6-8; Exodus 12:14-20; 1 Corinthians 5:7-8).
4. The Feast of Firstfruits (Leviticus 23:9-14; 1 Corinthians 15:20-23).

The verses to be memorized:

I am the LORD your God . . . observe all My statutes, and all My judgments, and do them: I am the LORD.
(Leviticus 19:36b, 37)

THE LESSON

Everybody loves a special day. What are some of the occasions which we celebrate? (Let students suggest some of the annual celebrations in your country. Discuss briefly *why* and *how* each is observed. Emphasize the fact that these days usually help us to remember a famous person or an event which happened in the past.)

Israel was God's special nation. Moses was God's appointed leader of His nation. Through Moses, God gave laws for the people to obey. God also explained:

1. How the people of Israel could come to Him through the blood of a sacrifice.
2. How they were to worship Him.
3. How they were to live each day to please Him.

God wanted His people to remember what He had done for them. So He said, "Moses, tell the people to observe *seven holy feasts*. Everybody must set aside these days each year. The people are to meet together and worship. They are to give thanks and praise for all I have done for them."

1. THE SABBATH
**Leviticus 23:1-3; Genesis 2:1-3;
Exodus 20:9-11; Nehemiah 13:15-18**

God continued, "Before you explain about the feasts, Moses, remind the people that the seventh day of each week is the Sabbath–a day of rest."

When did God first set aside the seventh day as a day of rest? (Review briefly Genesis 2:1-3.) He gave an example to the Israelites by "resting" on the seventh day after six days of creation.

Later God gave the Ten Commandments to Israel. He reminded His people that the seventh day of the week was the Sabbath of the Lord God. (Exodus 20:9-11.) God knew how easy it would be for His people to forget this. So again He commanded Moses, "Tell My people Israel that they must not do *any* work on the Sabbath. Instead, they shall rest. They are to remember the miracles I did to deliver them from slavery in Egypt." (See Deuteronomy 5:12-15.)

Show Illustration #1

At first, it was not hard for the people to obey this command. They did not do any work on the Sabbath day. Fathers gathered their families and reminded them of the miracles which God had done. (Review briefly Exodus 7-12.)

But as the years went by, the people forgot. They began to work on the Sabbath. (See Nehemiah 13:15-18.) What disobedience!

Wait a minute though. Before criticizing the Israelites, let me ask you a question. Do you give one day a week to God for rest and worship? Or do you use all seven days to work and play?

The Lord Jesus arose from the dead on Sunday, the first day of the week. Since then, the Christian's day of worship has been resurrection day–the first day of the week. (See Luke 24:1-7; Hebrews 10:25.) Do you honor the Lord on His day?

- 18 -

2. THE PASSOVER
Leviticus 23:4-5; Exodus 12:1-51; Deuteronomy 16:1-8

In addition to setting aside the Sabbath for God, the Israelites were to observe certain holy days. Through Moses, God gave instructions for His people. "In April each year, I want you to remember the night your eldest sons were protected in Egypt. This will be the *Feast of Passover*. When the destroyer saw the lamb's blood around each door, he passed over My people. But the Egyptians' sons were slain."

Show Illustration #2

God added, "Here is the way I want My people to remember this. Once a year each family is to kill a perfect male lamb just as the Israelites did that night in Egypt. Your children will ask, 'Why are we doing this?' Fathers must give this explanation: 'God saved all our firstborn sons when the destroyer passed through Egypt. Those who obeyed Him by sprinkling blood around their doors, were safe'."

Year after year the Israelites obediently observed the Feast of Passover as God had commanded. Thousands of lambs were killed. Then one day, almost 1,500 years after God had given these instructions, things were changed. The Lord Jesus Christ, the Lamb of God, was sacrificed for all the sins of the whole world. (See Luke 23:33, 46; 1 Corinthians 5:7; 1 Peter 1:18-19.) Since then, there has been no need to sacrifice lambs or any other animals. (See Hebrews 10:10-14.) Nor is there any reason now to observe the Feast of Passover. Because Christ, the perfect Lamb shed His own blood, those who trust in Him will escape eternal death. If you belong to Him, are you grateful for this? Does your life show your gratitude?

3. THE FEAST OF UNLEAVENED BREAD
Leviticus 23:6-8; Exodus 12:14-20; 1 Corinthians 5:7-8

After sprinkling the blood of the lambs on the doorposts, the Israelites went inside their homes. Each family roasted and ate the lamb which had been sacrificed to save the oldest son. They had their final meal in Egypt–eating the lamb with unleavened bread.

(*Teacher:* Explain that leaven is yeast which is mixed in bread dough to make it rise. The yeast causes the dough to ferment. It fills the dough with harmful bubbles of alcohol and carbon dioxide. When the bread is baked, these dangerous elements escape, leaving holes which make the bread lightweight. Unleavened bread is made *without* yeast and is flat.)

In the middle of the night, the Egyptians' sons died and their families were terrified. They begged God's people to leave their land at once. Immediately the Israelites grabbed their belongings and hurried toward the Red Sea.

God reminded Moses, "That night was the beginning of your new life under My direction. Do not let your children forget it. To help them remember, you must celebrate *the Feast of Unleavened Bread* each year in mid-April." Moses listened carefully. God explained exactly how the people were to observe this week-long holy occasion:

1. "Do not do any work except prepare food for your family on the first and last days of the holy observance.
2. "On those two days, everyone must meet together in a special service of thanksgiving and rejoicing.
3. "Every family must offer a sacrifice to Me on each of the seven days of the feast.
4. "Only unleavened bread may be eaten during the whole week. The people dare not even have yeast in their homes that week. Anyone who disobeys this command and eats bread made with yeast during this week, must be put out of the camp. He cannot have fellowship with My people." (See Exodus 12:19.)

Do you wonder why God was so particular about eating bread made without yeast?

In the Bible, leaven (yeast) is a reminder of evil because it causes things to ferment or spoil. (See Matthew 16:11-12; 1 Corinthians 5:7.) The bread with yeast was not evil. But it was to be an object lesson reminding Israel that as yeast ferments, so sin always spoils fellowship with God. Sin would have to be removed from their lives if they were to please their Father in Heaven.

Today we no longer celebrate the Feast of Unleavened Bread. But God reminds Christians of the same object lesson. (Read 1 Corinthians 5:7-8.) Sin is evil. Sin keeps us from obeying God.

Show Illustration #3

So God commands us to get the sin out of our lives (See 2 Corinthians 7:1.) just as the Israelites removed all the leaven from their houses. He wants our lives to be without evil, like the unleavened bread. (The round object in the illustration is a reminder of the flat, unleavened bread.)

And God wants us to read His Word, study it, and think about it. (See Psalm 119:9, 11, 18, 27, 105, 130.) By doing so, we become strong Christians who please the Lord God.

4. THE FEAST OF FIRSTFRUITS
Leviticus 23:9-14; 1 Corinthians 15:20-23

Another holy day was also to be observed in April. It was *the Feast of Firstfruits*. This was not a reminder of something which had happened in the past. It was a picture of a future event which we can understand better than could the Israelites! For it was a preview of Someone who would come later.

The people of Israel never planted gardens while they wandered in the wilderness. So they never reaped any crops. How did they get food to eat? (Review God's provision of manna and quails in Exodus 16.)

Looking forward to the time when their wanderings would be over and His people would be in the land He had promised them, God gave instructions to Moses. "When you reach the land to which I am leading you, plant gardens and fields. I will give you sunshine and rain. Your seeds will grow and you will reap fine crops. When the grain begins to ripen, go to the fields on the *first* day of the week (the day after the Sabbath)."

Show Illustration #4

God continued, "Cut a bundle of grain and take it to the priest. It is an offering of thanksgiving to Me *before* you yourself eat any of it."

These were the *firstfruits* of the harvest. This is why this holy day was called the Feast of Firstfruits. Plenty of grain and fruits would follow for the people. But the very first of the crops were to be given to God.

Now let us see what God teaches about today's Firstfruits. (*Teacher:* Have students read 1 Corinthians 15:20-23 in unison with you. If they cannot do so, you should read these verses slowly several times.)

Who is called the "Firstfruits" in these verses? *(Christ)* Fifteen hundred years after God announced the Feast of Firstfruits, Christ died. He, the Passover Lamb, did not stay on the cross. Nor did He stay in the tomb. On Sunday, the first day of the week–*the day after the Sabbath*–He arose from the dead! (Show top of illustration #4.) He was the *first* to rise from the dead and receive a resurrection body. This is why He is called the *Firstfruits*.

Because Christ arose, every person who trusts in Him as Saviour will also rise. When? When He comes in the air to take all believers to Heaven. (See 1 Corinthians 15:23; 1 Thessalonians 4:13-18.) This is the most glorious hope that anyone can have. Do you have this hope? Are you looking for His coming in the air?

God wanted the Israelites to remember all He had done for them. And He wants you to remember what He has done for you. Do you honor the Lord on His day? Do you live the kind of life that shows your gratitude to the Lamb of God? Do you turn from the leaven of sin, seeking to live a pure and holy life? Are you looking for the coming of the Lord Jesus in the air?

If you have to answer "no" to any of these questions, will you talk to God about it right now? List in your notebook what you must do to correct these faults immediately.

Lesson 2
THE FEASTS OF THE LORD (Part 2)

Scripture to be studied: Leviticus 23:15-44

The *aim* of the lesson: To show that the holy feasts pointed to past events and also to the future.

What your students should *know*: That God's Word is truth and what He has promised will be accomplished.

What your students should *feel*: Elated that God has a sovereign plan for His people.

What your students should *do*: Prepare for Christ's coming. Pray that Jewish people will turn to Jesus, their Messiah.

Lesson outline for the teacher's and students' notebooks:
1. The Feast of Pentecost (Leviticus 23:15-22; Acts 2:1-47).
2. The Feast of Trumpets (Leviticus 23:23-25; 1 Thessalonians 4:13-18).
3. The Day of Atonement (Leviticus 23:26-32).
4. The Feast of Tabernacles (Leviticus 23:33-44).

The verses to be memorized:

I am the LORD your God . . . observe all My statutes, and all My judgments, and do them: I am the LORD.
(Leviticus 19:36b, 37)

NOTE TO THE TEACHER

God knows how easy it is for people to forget Him. So He warned Israel about this. (See Deuteronomy 6:12-13.) And He set aside seven annual feasts as reminders of His care. As you teach, remember the two purposes of the feasts: (1) they were constant reminders to Israel of God–who He is and what He had done for them; (2) they are divine illustrations of the future program of God.

Depending upon the learning ability of your students, it may be necessary to develop two or three lessons from this one. Review *constantly* as you progress with the feasts.

THE LESSON

Do you remember what you did last year on this date? (Refer to today's date.) Can you remember what you did last month on this date? How quickly we forget!

Why did God command Israel to set aside seven holy feasts each year? (Encourage student response.)

The Israelites did not have Bibles as we do today. So they did not understand that their seven holy feasts also pictured future events in God's program. Since we have the whole Bible today, we know what these events are. (As you review the first three feasts, Show Illustrations from the first lesson. Mention the historical significance of the feasts and the future events which they illustrate.)

1. *THE PASSOVER:* a picture of Christ Jesus, the Passover Lamb who would die to redeem us–set us free–from sin.
2. *THE FEAST OF UNLEAVENED BREAD:* a reminder that sin spoils the believer's fellowship with God. God's children must read the Bible to grow into strong Christians, confessing sins which hinder fellowship with God, the holy One.
3. *THE FEAST OF FIRSTFRUITS:* a picture of Christ's resurrection from the dead. His resurrection assures us that we, too, shall rise from the dead.

The Israelites looked forward to the holy feast days. They did not work on those days. But they were not allowed to do as they pleased. God explained in detail exactly what they were to do on each special day.

Moses listened carefully to God's instructions. Later he would tell the Leaders of Israel what God commanded.

1. THE FEAST OF PENTECOST
Leviticus 23:15-22; Acts 2:1-47

God began, "Moses, count 50 days from the day you celebrate the Feast of Firstfruits. This will be your next holy day. It is *the Feast of Pentecost*."

Do you remember when the Feast of Firstfruits was held? *(In mid-April.)* So in what month would the Feast of Pentecost be held? (Help students to calculate that it would be in early June.)

God continued, "Moses, the Feast of Pentecost will come at the time the wheat is harvested. Each family must bake two loaves of wheat bread. These are to be taken to the Tabernacle and offered as a thanksgiving for My blessings. (See Deuteronomy 16:10..) With the loaves, bring animal sacrifices."

Why did the Israelites have to offer animal sacrifices when they worshiped God? *(Without shedding of blood they, sinners, could not be accepted by the holy God. See Leviticus 4:20; 17:11; Hebrews 9:22.)*

God added, "No one dare do any work on this holy day. Everyone must observe the Feast of Pentecost with great rejoicing. Your children will ask you why you are so happy. Tell them, 'We used to be slaves in Egypt. But God set us free to obey His laws instead.' (See Deuteronomy 16:12.)

The Israelites faithfully kept this day holy while they were in the wilderness. Later, they were living in the land God had given them. During that time, the men went to Jerusalem each year for the Feast of Pentecost. (See Acts 2:1, compare 20:16.) This they did for hundreds of years. The year that Christ died, rose, and ascended to Heaven, thousands were in Jerusalem for Pentecost. These Jewish men were from many countries. They did not believe that Jesus was God's Son. They refused to receive Him, the promised One sent from God. They were at the temple offering their loaves of bread made from the freshly harvested wheat. They were also offering their animal sacrifices–just as Moses had taught their people hundreds of years before.

But the disciples of Christ were not at the temple. They were in a house. Before the Lord Jesus had returned to Heaven, He had given them a command. "Go back to Jerusalem," He said. "Wait there for your Helper, the Holy Spirit, whom I shall send. He'll give you the courage and power to tell others of Me. (See Acts 1:8; compare John 14:16-17, 26; 16:7-15; Romans 8:26.)"

Show Illustration #5

So, on Pentecost, the disciples were obeying the Lord's command. They were waiting for the coming of the Spirit of God. Suddenly the Holy Spirit came down to live in those who believe in Jesus. (See John 14:17.) It was exactly 50 days after the Lord Jesus had risen from the dead! The Spirit's coming was announced by a roar, like wind. Tongues that looked like fire divided themselves and settled upon the head of each one. Each was given special power, as Christ had promised. They were able to speak languages which they had never studied. (To teach details, use last half of Lesson 2, NT Volume 14.)

Ever since that day, the Holy Spirit comes to live within the hearts of all true believers the moment they place their trust in Him. Because He is the Spirit of God, He can be everywhere at once.

He makes the believers into one big family–the family of God. God's family is known as *the church*. The church is made up of born again believers who have the Holy Spirit living in them. Believers may be either Jews or Gentiles. (Gentiles are those who are not Jews.)

Do you see why the Feast of Pentecost was observed with two loaves of bread made with leaven? The church of Christ which began on Pentecost is made up of two kinds of people–Jews and Gentiles. Although they have been saved from their sin by the Lord Christ, they are not sinless. (See 1 John 1:8.) The loaves of leaven are reminders that believers will always have their sin natures as long as they are here on earth. But they also have the Spirit of God within them. And if they let Him, He will lead them to do the things which please God.

The coming of the Holy Spirit was the one great Pentecost toward which God had been looking for 1,500 years.

2. THE FEAST OF TRUMPETS
Leviticus 23:23-25; 1 Thessalonians 4:13-18

During the time of Moses, God set aside still other holy observances. July, August, and September went by with no feast days. But in October there were three holy occasions. October began with the *Feast of Trumpets*. This was New Year's day to the Jewish people. (*Teacher:* If your culture observes New Year's day, discuss how it is celebrated.)

This was a happy day for the Israelites. The trumpets were sounded. No one worked. These Jewish people worshiped God and offered sacrifices. Afterwards, they spent the day feasting and thanking God for His goodness to them. (See Nehemiah 8:2, 9-12.)

At least two trumpets were blown. (*Teacher:* Study carefully the instructions concerning trumpets given in Numbers 10:1-10. The two silver trumpets were to be sounded for various reasons. Among these reasons, two are prominent: (1) the calling together of the assembly; (2) the announcement that the Israelites were to pack up and move.) Each trumpet sound was a reminder of something which had happened when the Israelites were in the wilderness. At the sound of one trumpet, the people were called together for a meeting. The sound of another trumpet meant they were to continue their journey to the land God had given them.

The Feast of Trumpets points forward to two events which have not yet taken place. But they will surely happen!

Show Illustration #6

1. One day–it could be soon–God's trumpet is going to sound. On that day the Lord Jesus will descend from Heaven in the clouds. Those who belong to Him and have already died, will be raised from the dead. They will be brought together with all believers who are still alive on earth. And all of them together will be caught up to meet the Lord in the air. What a meeting that will be!

(Point to arrow at left of illustration.) From then on, believers will always be together with the Lord. (See 1 Corinthians 15:51-53; 1 Thessalonians 4:16-17.)

Will you be among those who will meet the Lord in the air? You can be sure of it if you have placed your trust in Christ as your Saviour.

2. Seven years later, God's trumpet will sound again. And the Lord Jesus will come right down to earth. (Point to arrow on right and show lower part of illustration.) This time the sound of God's trumpet will call the Israelites to journey from all over the world back to Israel, their own land. (Read Matthew 24:29-31; compare Isaiah 18:3; 27:13; Joel 2:1–3:21.)

The feast of trumpets was a happy time. What a happy day it will be for the Jews when they are finally in their homeland!

3. THE DAY OF ATONEMENT
Leviticus 23:26-32

Right after the happy Feast of Trumpets was the Day of Atonement. (*Teacher:* Teach this section by reviewing lesson 4 of Volume 11.) This was the only feast day on which the people were sad. Why were they sad? (*They were sorry for their sins which came between them and God.*)

How did they receive forgiveness for their sins? (*The blood of the sin offering covered their sins.*) Who offered the sacrifices on the Day of Atonement? (*The high priest*) What special privilege did the high priest have on the Day of Atonement? (*This was the only day of the year he was allowed to enter the Most Holy Place in the Tabernacle. Here the presence of God dwelt above the mercy seat.*)

Why did the high priest use two goats for the sin offering on this day? (*One goat was killed. The high priest sprinkled its blood on and in front of the mercy seat in the Most Holy Place. When God saw the blood, He forgave the sins of the whole nation. The second goat carried the sins of the nation out into the wilderness. There, as the goat was lost and forgotten, God forgot the sins of the people. See Leviticus 16:1-34.*)

Is it necessary for us to celebrate the Day of Atonement today? Why not? (*Before Christ died, though hundreds of sacrifices were offered, they only covered the sins of the people* temporarily. More sacrifices were needed. But the blood of Christ constantly cleanses forever the sins of all who trust in Him.)

Today most Jewish people do not believe that Jesus Christ is the Son of God. They do not believe He shed His blood on the cross to pay the full penalty for sins.

Show Illustration #7

A day is coming when the LORD Jesus is coming back to rule the earth. Then when He reigns in power and glory, many Jews will repent. (See Matthew 24:30.) In that future day, as on the Day of Atonement, they will be sad and mourn. Why? Because they had rejected Christ. (See Zechariah 12:1-14.) At that time, a great number will turn to Him, believing that He is indeed the Son of God, their Saviour. And God promises that many Israelites will then be saved. (See Romans 11:26; Jeremiah 31:34; Hebrews 8:12; 10:16-17.)

4. THE FEAST OF TABERNACLES
Leviticus 23:33-44

Five days after the Day of Atonement, there was another holy observance. This was *the Feast of Tabernacles*. It lasted seven days.

During the 40 years the Israelites wandered in the wilderness, they lived in tents. They were led by God from place to place. They took down their tents and set them up again many times. God wanted them to remember their wanderings when they reached the promised land and lived in houses.

So in mid-October, each family was to cut branches of trees and make a shelter. Then the entire family moved into their shelter for seven days. What fun this must have been for the children! It was like going camping!

"Why are we doing this?" many asked their fathers.

"God wants us to remember how He led our people out of Egypt. He wants us to remember how we lived in tents and how He cared for us in the wilderness."

(*Teacher:* Review briefly God's provision of water and food for the Israelites, Exodus 15: 1-27; 16:1-36; 17:1-7. Also, how He provided protection against Amalek, Exodus 17:8-16. See Old Testament Volume 8, lessons 1, 2, 3.)

The Feast of Tabernacles was a holy time of great rejoicing for everyone. They all remembered God's goodness to them.

But a time of even greater rejoicing is coming for God's people, the Jews. We learned that the Lord Jesus is coming down to earth again. And the trumpet of God will call the Israelites back to Palestine. When they see Christ, many will finally believe that He is their Messiah, the Son of God.

Show Illustration #8

Then the Lord Jesus will be the Ruler over the whole earth for 1,000 years. (See Revelation 20:4, 6.) What a time of rejoicing that will be for the Jews living then!

Today there are many Jewish people who have never yet heard the Gospel. Write in your notebook the names of any Jews whom you know. Then let us ask God to give you an opportunity to introduce them to the Lord Jesus this week.

God has a wonderful future planned for all His people! If you are not His child, but will truly turn to Him today, you, too, can be a part of His wonderful future. Will you place all your trust in Him right now?

(*Teacher:* Conclude your lesson with an invitation and prayer. Then urge your students to bring to the next class session something which they have made for themselves.)

Lesson 3
REST AND LIBERTY

Scripture to be studied: Leviticus 25; verses cited in lesson

The *aim* of the lesson: To show that God's rules for governing the Israelites were for their own good.

   What your students should *know*: That because God was the Israelites' Creator, He had the right to govern them and their land.

   What your students should *feel*: An awareness of God's sovereign right over their lives and a desire to obey His commands.

   What your students should *do*: Submit to God's will and commands.

Lesson outline (for the teacher's and students' notebooks):
1. Rest for the land (Leviticus 25:1-7, 19-23).
2. Liberty for the people (Leviticus 25:8-18, 39-55).
3. God's judgment for disobedience (Leviticus 26:34-45; 2 Kings 24:1-25:30; 2 Chronicles 36:14-21).
4. Our liberty and rest (John 8:32-36; Hebrews 4:1-10).

The verses to be memorized:

   I am the LORD your God . . . observe all My statutes, and all My judgments, and do them: I am the LORD.
   (Leviticus 19:36b, 37)

NOTE TO THE TEACHER

Before teaching this lesson, review lesson #2 carefully. It is filled with important information about the past and future of the Israelites. The Word of God cannot be perfectly understood without a clear knowledge of God's program for the Jewish people.

Review, review, REVIEW!

THE LESSON

What did you bring to class today that you made for yourself? (Let students show what they brought and tell about it. Show something you made, too. Point out that because they made them, these articles belong to them. So they have the right to do with them as they please. If they let someone else use their article, they have the right to say how it must be cared for.)

Who made the earth? (See Genesis 1:1.) Then to whom does the earth belong? (Psalm 24:1, 1 Corinthians 10:26) Does this mean that God can do what He wants with the earth? (Discuss.)

Many hundreds of years ago, God led Abraham to the land of Canaan (often called Palestine and now called Israel). There God gave this promise: "Abraham, I am giving this land to you and to all your people who come after you. It will be yours forever." (See Genesis 17:8.)

God never changed this promise. Many from other lands have lived in Palestine. But it belongs to the Jews (Abraham's descendants). It will always be theirs in God's eyes, even if invaders occupy it from time to time. God has not given any other part of the earth to a particular nation. But remember, Israel is God's *special* nation.

God used a famine to lead Jacob (Abraham's grandson) and his family out of Canaan and down to Egypt. They lived there some 400 years. Then God led them back to their own land again.

He spoke to Moses who was from the family line (a descendant) of Jacob. "Moses, the land of Canaan (Palestine) is Mine," said God. "I have chosen to give it to My people, Israel. I have rules that the Israelites must obey in this land. These rules are for their own good. Be sure they understand My laws." (See Leviticus 25:23.)

1. REST FOR THE LAND
Leviticus 25:1-7, 19-23

Moses gathered the leaders of Israel together. Could their meeting have been something like this?

"Men, you know God is leading us back to the land of our fathers–Abraham, Isaac, and Jacob."

All the men nodded their heads.

Moses continued, "When we get there, each family will be given a piece of land to live on and to farm. God said you are to plant crops and reap harvests for six years. Then the seventh year you must let the land rest. You must not plant anything."

"What shall we eat if we do not plant anything that year?" the men asked.

Moses explained, "You have nothing to worry about. God promises to give you a big harvest the sixth year. In fact it will be so big that you will have enough to eat for three years! You shall have more than enough for the sixth year. There will be plenty for the seventh year when you do not plant the gardens. And enough will be left for the eighth year until you have another harvest. (See Leviticus 25:21.)"

"What should we do with the fruit that grows on the vines and trees during the seventh year?" asked one man.

"Whoever wants it may eat it, no matter on whose land it grows," answered Moses.

Another asked, "If we do not work in our fields what shall we do with our time?"

Show Illustration #9

Moses answered, "You will have more time to teach your children the law of God. Then they, too, will obey Him. (See Deuteronomy 31:10-13.)"

Each seventh year God wanted to provide for Israel without their working. They were simply to trust Him to care for them and obey Him.

2. LIBERTY FOR THE PEOPLE
Leviticus 25:8-18, 39-55

Moses continued to explain God's laws to the leaders of Israel.

"When you settle in the land of Canaan, the year of Jubilee will be a special year for you."

"What is the year of jubilee?" one of the men demanded.

"Every fiftieth year will be the year of jubilee," said Moses. "On the Day of Atonement that year, the trumpet will sound announcing a whole year of liberty and great joy for everyone."

"How will the year of jubilee differ from other years?" asked another.

Moses explained carefully. (#1) "First, you will not plant your fields. God will provide plenty of food for you just as He will each seventh year."

One man jumped to his feet. "That means we will not plant gardens for two consecutive years!" he exclaimed. "The forty-ninth year will be one of the seventh years when we let out land rest. And the fiftieth will be the year of jubilee. How will we ever be able to feed our families?"

Moses answered, "God has promised to provide an extra big harvest during the forty-eighth year. So you will have *plenty* to eat. He wants you to trust Him. He wants you to believe that He will keep His promise."

(#2) Moses continued. "During the forty-nine years before jubilee, some families might need money. To get it, they may sell their land or houses. In the year of jubilee, the things they had sold will be turned back to them."

(#3) "But most important of all, *liberty for all the people* will be proclaimed in the year of jubilee," exclaimed Moses.

"Liberty? Why must liberty for all the people be proclaimed?" the leaders asked. "We *have* liberty! We are not slaves. We *are* free!"

"Yes, yes!" Moses assured them. "You are free. But there will be people who will owe debts which they cannot pay. When that happens, they may go to the man to whom they owe the money and say, 'I have no money to pay my debt. I will be your servant. I will work for you until all that I owe you is paid'."

"Sometimes people will be so poor that they will not have enough to eat. They may go to someone who is rich and say, 'I will be your servant if you will give my family and me a place to live, food to eat, and clothing to wear'."

"From then on, that man will not be free. He will be a servant and work hard for his master. He will be given only what he needs (2 Kings 4:1)."

Show Illustration #10A

Moses explained, "In the year of jubilee, however, all debts will be canceled and forgotten.

Show Illustration 10B

And all servants will be set free."

What a wonderful year jubilee would be! Everyone would have a fresh start–a new beginning!

God really loved His people, the Israelites. He wanted them to have a good life in their own land. His rules were perfect. If they would obey His commands, they would be wonderfully happy.

3. GOD'S JUDGMENT FOR DISOBEDIENCE
Leviticus 26:34-45; 2 Kings 24:1-25:30; 2 Chronicles 36:14-21

Forty years went by before the Israelites reached the land God had given them. By then, Moses had died. And Joshua was their leader. He divided the land among all the families, exactly as God had commanded.

Each family worked hard to clear off the weeds, dig up the soil, and plant seeds. God sent the rain and sunshine. And their crops grew. How happy the people were with the good harvest God gave them!

Six years went by. When it was time to let the land rest, no one remembered! How could they forget when God had been so good to them?

The people of God made friends with the people in Canaan who did not worship the true God. These people did not let their land lie idle. The Jews forgot God's laws. They forgot to teach their children God's commandments.

Show Illustration #11A
Year after year went by. God sent preachers to warn that He would punish them if they did not obey Him. But they would not listen (2 Chronicles 36:15-16). God was patient for many, many years. Then He let the people of Babylon defeat the Israelites.

Show Illustration #11B
The Babylonians took the Israelites to Babylon and kept them as prisoners of war for 70 years (2 Chronicles 36:16, 18).

For those 70 years the land could rest as God had planned. (See Leviticus 26:34-35, 43; 2 Chronicles 36:21.) The Israelites now knew that God meant exactly what He said. They understood that forgetting God is evil (Jeremiah 2:19). They learned too late that God punishes disobedience.

The people cried. "If only we had listened to God! If only we had remembered His rules! If only we had obeyed Him!"

But it was too late. They were captives of foreigners. They could not live as free people as God had planned.

4. OUR LIBERTY AND REST
John 8:32-36; Hebrews 4:1-10

We have been talking about rules which God gave to Israel long ago when they were about to move into the land He promised them. Now we are going to think about some of God's commands for us today.

#1 The Lord Jesus says, "You shall know the truth, and the truth shall make you free." (See John 8:32.) This is a commandment of God. (Repeat with the students until the verse is memorized.)

Maybe you are thinking, "I *am* free. I am not a slave. I do not need to be made free!"

Jesus' answer is, "Whoever commits (practices) sin is the servant (slave) of sin." (See John 8:34.)

Who commits sin? (Encourage discussion. Base conclusions on Romans 3:23, emphasizing ALL.) All have sinned. This includes you and me. We do not choose to become *slaves* of sin. We are born this way. (See Psalm 51:5; Romans 3:10-12.)

How can we be made free? "If the Son therefore shall make you free, you shall be free indeed." (See John 8:36.) Who is the Son? (*Jesus Christ*)

Show Illustration #12
How can you and I be set free by Jesus Christ? By trusting in Him who gave His precious blood on the cross. We are bought with a price! There is no other way to be free.

God promises everlasting life with Him in Heaven for all who are made free by Jesus Christ. But He also warns of everlasting punishment in hell for everyone who refuses to trust His Son as Saviour. (See John 3:18, 36.)

Israel disobeyed God. They learned too late that God meant what He said. Will you, too, wait until it is too late? Or will you accept Christ today?

#2 God also commands us to *rest* and *trust* in Him (Hebrews 4:1, 10). Does resting and trusting mean working hard? NO! Yet how hard people *work* trying to be good enough for God to let them enter Heaven! (Discuss some things people do in your country to seek to please God: attending church, visiting shrines, burning candles, giving money, observing days, etc.)

God sees what people do and He says, "All your righteousness are as filthy rags (Isaiah 64:6)!"

Are you trying to be good enough to get to Heaven? You never will be good enough! The only way to be good enough is to believe on the Lord Jesus Christ (Acts 16:31). Place all your trust in Him. By His death and resurrection He has done all that God requires. He wants you simply to trust in Him and in what He has done.

These are God's rules. They are for our good. He has created us. He loves us. Will you choose today to obey Him and enjoy His blessing?

Lesson 4
BLESSING OR JUDGMENTS

NOTE TO THE TEACHER

In the long ago, God gave the Israelites a choice. If they would obey His commands, He promised to give them great earthly blessings. If they disobeyed Him, they would be punished. They chose to disobey God. And today, hundreds of years later, they are still suffering chastisement for their wrong choice. Even so, God has chosen the Israelites as His special people. So a day will come when many will turn to Christ. And God will restore them to their land. Then He will bless them according to His promise.

We, too, have a free will. We have the ability to make choices. But it is sobering to remember that we who believe in Christ must all stand before His judgment seat. There our works will be judged by Him, the righteous Judge (See 2 Corinthians 5:10). Whatever we sow, we shall reap (See Galatians 6:7-8). Are your choices according to the will of God, teacher? If so, your life will be a good example to your students.

Scripture to be studied: Leviticus 26; Deuteronomy 28; verses cited in lesson.

The *aim* of the lesson: To show that God gave Israel a choice which would affect their lives.

What your students should *know*: That in spite of Israel's wrong choice, God has a future program for His people.

What your students should *feel*: The seriousness of having a free will with which to choose whom they will serve and obey.

What your students should *do*: Choose today to serve God and obey Him.

Lesson outline for the teacher's and students' notebooks:

1. A warning against idols (Leviticus 26:1-2).
2. Blessings for obedience (Leviticus 26:3-13; Deuteronomy 28:1-14).
3. Curses for disobedience (Leviticus 26:14-39; Deuteronomy 28:15-68).
4. Israel's failure and future hope (Leviticus 26:40-45; Jeremiah 23:7-8; 30:3; 31:33-34).

The verses to be memorized:

I am the LORD your God . . . observe all My statutes, and all My judgments, and do them: I am the LORD.
(Leviticus 19:36b, 37)

The conversation of Phinehas and his father is of course, imaginary. Moses received the commands from God and gave them to the leaders. They, in turn, shared them with fathers. And fathers taught these truths to their families–just as fathers today should teach God's Word to their children.

THE LESSON

Today we are going to talk about making choices–something we all do every day.

This morning you chose to get up instead of staying in bed. You chose to come to this class. Some chose not to come. What other choices did you make today? (Encourage response.)

Whenever we make a choice, something happens. Good things happen when we make right choices. Bad things can come when we make wrong choices.

Long, long ago the Israelite people had to make an important choice. They could make a right choice or a wrong choice. Which would they choose?

The people of Israel were special to God. He had chosen them for Himself. He had wonderful plans for them. The Lord Jesus Christ, God's very own Son, was going to be born into one of the Israelite families! Through Him, all the nations in the world would be blessed. (See Genesis 12:3.) God longed for the Israelites to love Him and to obey Him.

They were on their way to the land God had promised them. God wanted His people to remember that He was their Ruler. He did not want them to forget all He had done for them. As we have seen in previous lessons, God gave them many commands.

God wanted the children as well as the parents to understand and obey His laws. Moses, therefore, explained God's instructions to the leaders. They were to go home and tell their families all that God commanded.

Phinehas, a little Israelite boy, would have listened carefully as his father explained that God had made a covenant with them.

"Father, what is a covenant?" asked Phinehas.

"A covenant is an agreement, Phinehas. Suppose I promised to give you a new slingshot if you would milk our cows every day for a week. This is a covenant. If you keep your part of the agreement, you get the slingshot. If you do not milk the cows every day, you have broken the covenant. And you will not get the slingshot."

1. A WARNING AGAINST IDOLS
Leviticus 26:1-2

Phinehas's father continued, "God has commanded that we are not to worship any kind of idols or images."

Show Illustration #13

Phinehas remembered the day when Moses was up the mountain talking to God. The Israelites had become impatient and asked Aaron to make an idol for them. (Review the incident of Exodus 32 by questioning your students. See Old Testament Volume 9, Lesson 2.)

"God was angry with us that day, wasn't He, Father?" asked Phinehas.

"Yes, He was very angry. And He had a right to be. We deliberately disobeyed Him by worshiping an idol we had made with our hands," his father said quietly. "Three thousand men died that day because of our great sin."

Phinehas silently thought about how serious it is to disobey God.

His father continued. "Many people living in the new land to which we are going, worship idols and images."

"Why do they worship something they make with their own hands?" asked Phinehas. "People are more powerful themselves than the images they make. How can they trust in a piece of wood or stone which cannot hear, or see, or help them?"

"Because they do not trust in our living God," his father answered. "Satan blinds them. They do not see how foolish it is to worship such things. But God knows that when we get in their land, we, too, will be tempted to worship idols. He constantly reminds us that He is our God. He commands, 'Do not forget the Sabbaths and feast days. Do not neglect the tabernacle and the offerings. Remember My commandments. These will remind you of all I have done for you. And you will not be tempted to make idols and worship them'."

2. BLESSINGS FOR OBEDIENCE
Leviticus 26:3-13; Deuteronomy 28:1-14

"Is that our part of the covenant?" asked Phinehas.

"Yes. God has given us laws so we know how to worship Him. He has explained that we are to live to please Him. He expects us to know these laws and obey them."

"Then what is His part of the covenant?" Phinehas wanted to know.

"He has promised us many good things IF we do what He commands. (1) He will send rain to water our gardens. He will give us so much to eat that we will have plenty left over when it is time to plant the gardens again. (2) There will be no war. Our enemies will be afraid of us. (3) God will chase away the wild animals that could harm us. (4) He will give us many children."

Show Illustration #14

"(5) And best of all, HE WILL DWELL AMONG US in the Tabernacle. He will be our God and we will be His people. We will not be slaves anymore to anybody!" Father became more and more enthusiastic as he told of the blessings God had promised.

3. CURSES FOR DISOBEDIENCE
Leviticus 26:14-39; Deuteronomy 28:15-68

"What will happen if we do not obey God's laws?" Phinehas asked.

Father sat quietly thinking for a long time before he answered. He spoke solemnly. "I hope that will never happen. God has warned of terrible punishments for us if we disobey Him. We must never forget that God is just. He is as faithful in punishing sin as He is in blessing obedience. IF we ignore Him and we do not listen and obey Him, He has warned us that (1) He will send locust plagues to eat up our crops. (2) He will not send rain for our gardens. Everything will dry up and the trees will not bear fruit. (3) He will let enemies rule over us. (4) He will send terrible sickness upon us. (5) He will send wild beasts to kill our children and animals."

Show Illustration #15

Phinehas's father continued, "If we insist on worshiping idols and forgetting the feast days and years of rest for the land, (6) God will let our enemies come in and take us away captive to their lands. We shall be out of the land which God wants us to have. We shall be separated from each other. We shall no longer live together as a nation under God's rule. He will not longer dwell among us in the Tabernacle."

What a solemn covenant God had made with His people!

Israel had a choice to make. Suppose you had been with them as they moved into the land of Canaan. What choice would you have made? (Let students discuss.)

4. ISRAEL'S FAILURE AND FUTURE HOPE
Leviticus 26:40-45; Jeremiah 23:7-8; 30:3; 31:33-34

God gave the Israelites the freedom to choose whom they would follow. (Read Deuteronomy 30:15-20 to the students slowly and distinctly. Question them to be sure they understand.)

I wish I could tell you that the Israelites always obeyed God and enjoyed His wonderful blessings. Instead, the Bible records something sad. When they arrived in the promised land of Canaan, they disobeyed God. They did not destroy all the wicked people there as God had commanded.(See Deuteronomy 20:16-18.) Rather, they lived among them. Soon the people God had chosen for Himself were bowing down to images of wood and stone. They worshiped false gods. Think of that!

God was patient with them. He sent prophets to warn them. Sometimes they listened for a while. But then they would forget. Hundreds of years went by. The Israelites paid no attention to their part of the covenant. God could not simply forget their sin. He kept warning them. "If you refuse to obey Me, you will be conquered by your enemies. They will take you to foreign countries as slaves." This is exactly what happened. The Israelites suffered because of their wrong choice. Great numbers were treated cruelly and killed by their enemies.

Even today, the Israelites (also called Jews) are scattered in every country of the world. Until some 30 years ago, they did not even have a country. Since then (1948), many Jews have been in their own land, Israel. But they still refuse to believe that the Lord Jesus Christ is the Son of God.

Show Illustration #16

Do you think God has forgotten them? No indeed! One day, when Jesus returns to earth, great numbers of them will repent. They will enter the 1,000 year millennial kingdom which Christ will set up on earth. The Lord will bring them back to their land and rule over them righteously. Jesus will be the perfect King. And for the first time, this world will have a perfect government. (See Ezekiel 37:21-28.)

What will it be like on the earth during the 1,000 year millennium? God will send plenty of rain so there will again be big harvests. The people will be safe in their own country. Neither their enemies nor wild beasts will be able to harm them. The people will not be hungry or sick. Every wrong will be immediately punished by Jesus Christ, the King. There will be peace in the whole world for the entire 1,000 years. What a glorious time that will be! (See Ezekiel 34:23-31; Isaiah 35:5-6; 9:6; 32:1.) "The earth shall be full of the knowledge of the Lord." (See Isaiah 11:9.)

Where will you be during that time? If you truly belong to the Lord Christ, you will be on earth ruling with Him for the 1,000 years. (See Revelation 20:6.) Between now and then, will you choose to obey Him? What does He want you to do for Him this week? List in your notebook the things He has asked you to do. Determine exactly how you plan to obey Him.

If you refuse to trust in the Lord, you will be separated from God. To be separated from God means to suffer His punishment in the lake of fire forever. Why? Because you failed to make the right choice concerning His Son, Jesus Christ. Will you confess your sin to God right now and receive Christ as your Saviour?

www.ingramcontent.com/pod-product-compliance
Lightning Source LLC
Chambersburg PA
CBHW060805090426
42736CB00002B/159